TIME FOR KIDS READERS

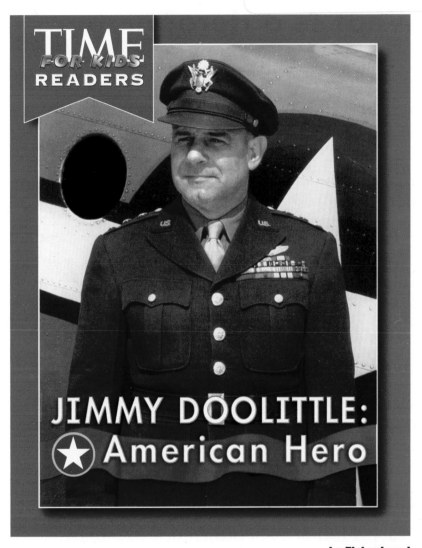

JIMMY DOOLITTLE:
 ★ American Hero

by Elaine Israel

⬢ Harcourt
SCHOOL PUBLISHERS

Orlando   Austin   New York   San Diego   Toronto   London

Visit *The Learning Site!*
www.harcourtschool.com

What Is a Hero?

When you think of a hero, who do you think of? Some people might think of firefighters, who risk their lives to save others and to put out fires. To some, heroes are rescue workers, who search through rubble after an earthquake. Others think of people who go about their lives in spite of physical challenges. Some heroes are people who fought for civil rights, for better working conditions, or for a cleaner environment.

Our nation's history is filled with acts of heroism, or courage. A hero inspires others in times of war and in times of peace. Honest . . . courageous . . . smart. These words all describe a Californian named Jimmy Doolittle. He was a true American hero.

Doolittle stands next to his biplane in 1929. A biplane is an airplane that has two sets of wings, one on top of the other.

North to Alaska, and South Again

Rosa and Frank Doolittle lived in Alameda, California, with their son James Harold, whom they called Jimmy. In 1896, gold was discovered in Alaska. Thousands of people rushed there. Frank Doolittle was among them.

In 1900 Frank Doolittle sent for his family. He had settled in the growing town of Nome, Alaska. Though he didn't find gold, he had found success as a carpenter.

Nome, Alaska, in the early 1900s

When Jimmy was seven years old, his family moved to Los Angeles, California.

As Jimmy went through school, he became interested in airplanes. He built motor-driven gliders. The gliders taught him a lot about flight.

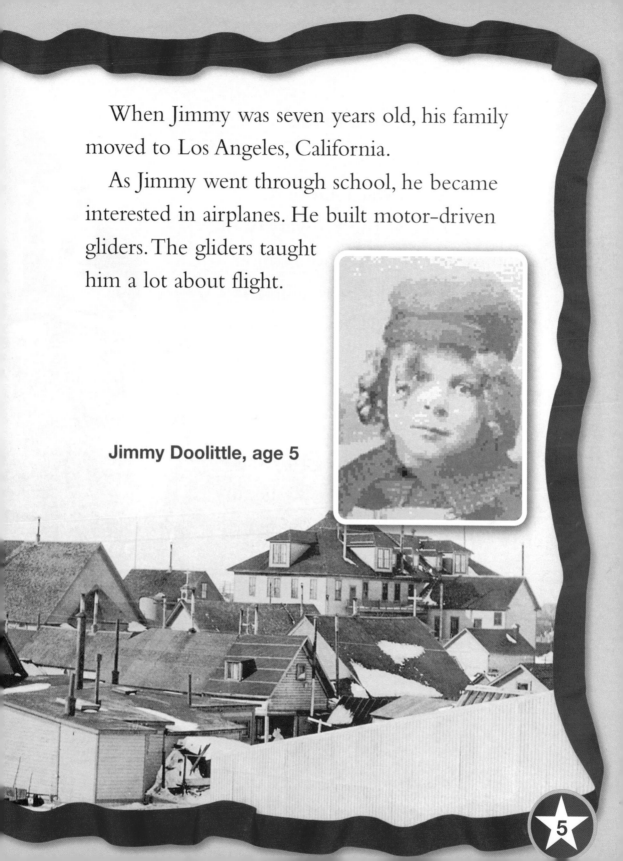

Jimmy Doolittle, age 5

Ups and Downs

In 1917 the United States entered World War I. Doolittle was a junior at the University of California. He left school to join the Army Signal Corps, where he learned how to fly. Doolittle then spent the rest of the war teaching others how to fly.

When the war was over, Doolittle stayed in the Army but also returned to school. He became an expert on the science of flying. He was the first to fly a plane from the East Coast to the West Coast in less than a day. He was the first to take off, fly, and land an airplane entirely by instruments.

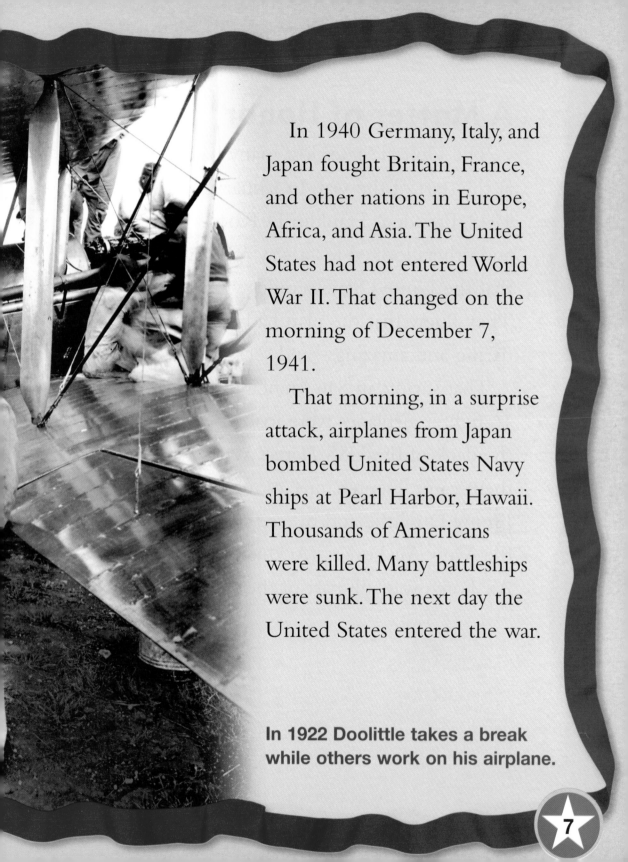

In 1940 Germany, Italy, and Japan fought Britain, France, and other nations in Europe, Africa, and Asia. The United States had not entered World War II. That changed on the morning of December 7, 1941.

That morning, in a surprise attack, airplanes from Japan bombed United States Navy ships at Pearl Harbor, Hawaii. Thousands of Americans were killed. Many battleships were sunk. The next day the United States entered the war.

In 1922 Doolittle takes a break while others work on his airplane.

A Matter of Honor

The United States lost many battles at the start of the war. In January 1942, President Franklin D. Roosevelt and others looked for a way to prove that the United States could win. They knew that the plan had to be daring and amazing—and secret.

That spring, in San Francisco Bay, 16 fighter airplanes were loaded onto the deck of the USS *Hornet*. With them came Lieutenant Colonel Jimmy Doolittle and his crews from the Army Air Forces. (At this time the Air Force was still part of the Army.)

This was the plan. The *Hornet* would sail within 400 miles of Tokyo, the capital of Japan. The bombers would take off from the deck of the ship. (That had never been done before.) The ship would then make a fast getaway. Jimmy Doolittle and his crews would bomb cities deep in the heart of Japan.

The bombers were supposed to drop their bombs at night. Then the fliers would head to nearby China, another country that was fighting Japan.

Bombers on the USS *Hornet* are ready to be flown in a raid on Japan in 1942.

But it didn't work out that way. The ship was far from Japan when a mighty storm blew in. Strong winds tossed around the huge *Hornet*. And to make matters worse, enemy ships were in the area. Would they send radio warnings home to Japan?

Doolittle and other officers decided that the bombers must not wait. They would fly in daytime.

The Japanese had been warned, but they didn't defend themselves in time. Doolittle's raid was a success.

In the United States, news of the raid sent the nation's spirits way up. Thanks to Doolittle and his Tokyo Raiders, the nation had its honor back.

Doolittle (first row, fourth from left) and some of his Tokyo Raiders are shown with Chinese officers who helped them.

Doolittle felt terrible because he had lost some of his crew. When the President ordered him to the White House, Doolittle thought he was in trouble. Not so! The President awarded Doolittle the Congressional Medal of Honor, one of the nation's highest awards. It was for leadership "beyond the call of duty." The other Tokyo Raiders were also honored.

Doolittle went right back into action. After all, there was still a war to be won. He led bombing raids on Germany. He hit enemy targets in North Africa. He returned to the Pacific and again attacked Japan. "He inspired thousands of people in every walk of life," said a friend.

Doolittle's wife, Jo, stands next to him as President Roosevelt presents him with the Congressional Medal of Honor.

Forever a Patriot

World War II ended in 1945. Doolittle retired from the military in 1959. His combat days were over, but he continued to serve his country. He never stopped testing and improving airplanes.

General James H. Doolittle died in 1993, at the age of 96, at his son's home in California. "He was an uncommon man," said the Tokyo Raiders at his funeral. "He was a man of wisdom and wit [humor], compassion and concern. . . . He was a patriot in the fullest sense of the word."

What did Doolittle hope to achieve in his life? A friend said that "it was simply a matter of trying to leave the earth a better place than he found it."

World War II Medal of Honor Winners Born in California

Daniel Judson Callaghan (Navy)

Edward A. Carter, Jr. (Army)

Ralph Cheli (Army Air Corps)

Clarence Byrle Craft (Army)

James Harold Doolittle (Army)

John William Finn (Navy)

Harold Gonsalves (U.S. Marine Corps)

David M. Gonzales (Army)

John Druse "Bud" Hawk (Army)

Joe Hayashi (Army)

Herbert Charpoit Jones (Navy)

Sadao S. Munemori (Army)

Kiyoshi K. Muranaga (Army)

Joe Nishimoto (Army)

Kazuo Otani (Army)

Ted T. Tanouye (Army)

Robert M. Viale (Army)

Ysmael R. Villegas (Army)

David Crowder Waybur (Army)